D1289658

KAYLEB RAE CANDRILLI

WHAT RUNS OVER

YESYES BOOKS, PORTLAND

COVER ART: "HELPLESS" BY YUTHA ADIPUTRA YAMANAKA
COVER & INTERIOR DESIGN: ALBAN FISCHER

ISBN 978-1-936919-35-2

PRINTED IN THE UNITED STATES OF AMERICA

PUBLISHED BY YESYES BOOKS
1614 NE ALBERTA ST
PORTLAND, OR 97211
YESYESBOOKS.COM

KMA SULLIVAN, PUBLISHER
JILL KOLONGOWSKI, MANAGING EDITOR
STEVIE EDWARDS, SENIOR EDITOR, BOOK DEVELOPMENT
ALBAN FISCHER, GRAPHIC DESIGNER
COLE HILDEBRAND, SENIOR EDITOR, OPERATIONS
BEYZA OZER, DEPUTY DIRECTOR OF SOCIAL MEDIA
AMBER RAMBHAROSE, CREATIVE DIRECTOR OF SOCIAL MEDIA
PHILLIP B. WILLIAMS, COEDITOR IN CHIEF, *VINYL*
AMIE ZIMMERMAN, EVENTS COORDINATOR
JOANN BALINGIT, ASSISTANT EDITOR
MARY CATHERINE CURLEY, ASSISTANT EDITOR
CARLY SCHWEPPE, ASSISTANT EDITOR, *VINYL*
HARI ZIYAD, ASSISTANT EDITOR, *VINYL*

CONTENTS

once on the back porch my lab barked / 1

If you live on top / 5

After rain there was always fire / 6

Tori tapped and her feet were a blur / 7

in the beginning / 8

My daddy's addiction / 9

Anything can be stolen / 11

We spend the years on the mountain / 12

At the house in Montrose / 13

Robbery is an open door / 14

Daddy says: Unzip the fucker / 15

When I was younger, I would machete / 17

I collect my daddy's sharp shot bats / 18

i spent my childhood lighting myself on fire / 19

i screamed undress me / 21

Many things prove hereditary / 22

I wondered at the rock cuts / 23

We were on the way out / 25

Homeschooled, I watched the towers / 27

My family prepared for the apocalypse / 28

When we got our first mountain / 29

My father's mother told me / 30

I have nothing / 31

my daddy, in the business / 32

In the beginning / 33

At a museum that spiral staircases / 34

Velvet grows on antlers / 36

when i killed my first buck / 38

the t-ball team blonde boy / 39

Because my father's mother is a witch / 40

I only fall in love / 41

I want to be the witch of Endor / 42

Back Mountain Dance Studio / 43

Tunkhannock Softball Bleachers / 44

At night I ride / 45

the 911 operator asks me / 46

When my daddy caught his cold / 47

Mountains form below the surface / 48

From the back seat / 50

I imagine my daddy's mind / 52

She says / 53

my mother was good at cooking birds / 54

In the 50s / 55

The neighbor boy and I hunted dragons / 56

Things try to crawl out / 57

me and tori licked food stamps / 58

In early Autumn I'd fire / 59

i spent years sticking my tongue / 60

Daddy played chicken / 62

let's imagine / 63

put a collar on me / 65

in the house on the hill / 66

planetary the way my partner moves / 67

When me and the one | 68

When they die | 69

The fact | 70

I want to write | 71

i say crucify me | 72

If I am too vainglorious | 73

what if, somewhere | 74

I collect holy books | 75

my boy tits | 76

when my lipstick is blue | 77

the hair mounding between my legs | 78

I catch lymphomania and roll | 79

I collect antique photographs | 80

When my mother chewed off | 81

as a child I made lists | 83

At the base | 84

to understand the scope | 86

I went back | 88

my daddy who art | 89

On the mountain | 90

The last deer I reach | 92

Acknowledgments | 95

for my mother.

once on the back porch my lab barked
and barked.
                he was always spooked
          by something, garter snake, black
snake, rabbit.
             daddy didn't ever
like it when dogs did what they do.

                  so when
my dog barked on the back porch
daddy brought a gun
                  and when he took
aim   i jumped in front and when he lifted
the safety   i was still right in front
and for minutes
           neither of us moved.

my daddy almost pumped me full
of lead.   my daddy almost   left me
for
          so ask me why i hate animals

and i'll answer with a trigger warning.
i'll say   *your dog*
        reminds me of daddy

If you live on top
of a mountain, things hit you
in migratory waves:

                              ravens,   lightning,   fire, fire
                                    flies,   monarchs.   They take over.

The lightning-struck trees smoke
like cigarettes in May,

                              black outs,

big-battered flash lights, big candles,
              your mother and father having hot
              wax sex upstairs.
                              They listen to Seal when this happens.
                              D-battered CD player spinning.

Outside, the roads that wind around the mountain
give way, fall
                    into themselves.   Think moat.

Another sink hole in Margret's   Hollow.

Every road around this town is named

                                                        Something

Hollow.

After rain there was always fire
newts everywhere. Slash burn saunter.
Amphibious and useless.

I would collect them with my sister Tori. Pinch them about the
middle and drop them into old beach buckets, the left over
sand on the bottom drying out their bellies—snails in salt. We
never knew better.

We piled them on top of one another, half gallon of fire—
writhe. After hours of collecting, we would spill them out
somewhere new, watch them slash burn through

                                        moss mountains.

We made refugees of them.
Our fingers soured with their urine.

//

Tori tapped and her feet were a blur / of music. At
her dance / competitions, I carried props / and rolls
of masking tape / on my arms like Bengal bracelets. /

//

The girls in my sister's troupe threw / their legs in the
air for me / and I striped the bottoms / of their taps
with tape. I couldn't let / them fall, slip on those fake
hard / wood floors.

//

My sister was the best / in the tri-state area. I filled /
grocery bags with trophies and ribbons. / I was
always there. Until

//

I grew older and hid / in other women's hotel
rooms, let / a rival choreographer / tack me up
against a wall, push / her breasts into my mouth,
where / I sucked and sucked, / her nipples tasting
like glue and rhinestones / and all the same / old
Frank Sinatra songs.

//

in the beginning
i reached
my hand
between
the legs
of a woman
who wouldn't
yet call
herself a woman
and she came
bloodstream
rhinestones
into my palm
she said *see*
rubies

My daddy's addiction
comes to me in a dream

and I beach on a dirty pond's
shore. Reeds and cattails tangle me.

The spaces between my spread fingers
make perfect scalene triangles and invite

water snakes. Three rhinestoned bodies
emerge in the webbing of my hand,

and they sink teeth
into the soft tissue.

Fire beneath my skin tattoos
from the inside out, purple-

green flames lick through the maps
of my veins. Wind blows

and water laps against my body.
My fingers—now the heads

of snakes—fight among themselves
before my mother brings the chiseled

shovel down hard—again and again, fingers
of venom writhe deep into black silt.

Anything can be stolen.

Semantics.

Klepto. Clepto. Kalypso. Calypso.

Maniac. Is what I was,

what they called me.

I kept one hand in a woman

the other in a cash drawer.

When a woman

I loved wanted to leave

I asked as my daddy did:

how will you live?

And they had no answers

but ruby red come and tears.

We spend the years on the mountain periscoping
in pine trees for flumes of smoke, for black
tailspin tornados. Every time a house
around goes up in flames I wonder
if my daddy lit the match and blew
fire, drought in the back
of his throat, kindling
tongue, gasoline
on his breath.

My mother collects marble: Apollo's head, birdbath,
gravestone, stampede of gargoyles through tall
grass. She yells at the sky when it drops
lightninged branches, bolts she clears
from the yard. From my bedroom
window, her arms look,
as if they hold a bundle
of sage and she burns,
she burns the broken
spirits away.

At the house in Montrose my mother, as a young girl, herded
peacocks through the pool house and checked the flair
of their plumage against bluer waters.
Now, a million years later, she says

they are heirloom

birds,

as she fluffs our Christmas trees with their tail feathers,
says *look at how the lights*

make them kaleidoscope.

When she talks about the pool house
she ticks off species on her fingers: peacocks,
roosters, the dogs: Lance and Rockie.
She talks about wolf
spiders, fist-sized
and spun through the portholes.

Robbery is an open   door
and my mother tells   the story of her quarter

collection heisted, all bicentennials,
colonial drummers   drumming.

At the laundromat, as a child, I'd seek them   out

of the change machine, slip   them into my mother's
palm.

She'd smile, because our laundromat had a cross
breeze.
and I had a way
of bringing everything back.

Daddy says: Unzip the fucker. Skin it fast.

Split its lips. Its eyelids.

Size up its skull so you can brag.

Cut the bullets out of its flesh if you can. Mementos.

Spit on its carcass as it burns. You won.

Lay it all out, somewhere dry.

Kneeling on the inside of its skin, scrape with a putty knife.

Smooth it like concrete.

Don't tear through to the hair. It's hard to patch up dead skin.

Salt. Borax. Rub it into the white. Kill the stink.

Use tape measure from toolbox. Ass to nose. Paw to paw.

Order glass eyes, foam skull, plastic mouth, ear liners.

Use mom's quilting pattern paper. Trace out the bear.

Use that shape for fluff and felt.

Use carpet padding if you've got some lying around.

Sew it all together, loop stitch, quick but tight.

Paint everything that doesn't look quite right.

Hang the fucker from the banister.

When I was younger, I would machete through the woods, pretend that sliced blackberries speckled my blade with blood. I wanted to spook deer. Light rain was the best time for this, deadening my footfalls. When I came upon them, I would run like mad, brandish what, in my mind, had become a cutlass—my hollering hung in the heavy, wet air. Deer scattered. The dry-warm patches looked stark and colorless against soaked ground. Where they had lain, I laid.

I hold a dulled machete over my daddy when he sleeps.

He opens his eyes and says nothing, goes back

to bed. He doubts my conviction. I know,

because that's what he says in the morning.

i spent my childhood lighting myself on fire

burns bubbling then breaking
open
poxed tom boy
still picking

arms and legs and face all opened up to the outside
all opened up to the dirt I rubbed there

the doctors called it *wound interference*
the doctors called it *excoriation disorder*
the doctors said *stop it, you'll scar*
you're scarring all over

pile of tough skin
call it *armored flesh*

my daddy said with narcotic
snow
ploughed
to the corners
of his mouth
you look like a fucking meth head

i screamed undress me from that dress
and my father's mother pulled

her voodoo doll out   showed me to push
pushpins through   my breasts

outside, garter snakes mate orgiastic
and male snakes gender switch

they hide from hawks this way   my envy
takes flame and   burns their scales

i know i came from clean birth
but I feel a mix of ash and soil sex

i cough penises and stick them to my pelvis
my salvation is voodoo pricks into my split

i want to be a snake
i want to be born again

i'm stabbing myself
for a fix

Many things prove hereditary and I can list them:
Coarse dark hair. Diabetes. Heroin addiction. Adultery.

A fear of both fresh and salt water. And imagine
how each is identified: tweezers, artificial sugars, glinting

syringes, wet lovers, my daddy just watching the tide
as it towed me out, and out, and out. The family tree

is not aquatic but I took my money and bought a one-piece
of Bluefin scales and gold leaf, which weighs heavy

and sinks fast. I dressed and it held me tightly;
it wasn't going to let a thing spill, and in that way

I was a fish before swimming; gills
ready for the water that I never had a chance

to taste. The pool house burnt the day I decided to learn
to swim. It burnt up and billowed curdled plastic,

all those lane dividers browned like marshmallows
over a fire I was taught to start.

I wondered at the rock cuts we drove through. I asked Daddy how they sliced the stone, I said *looks like God stuck a fork in it.*

But Daddy cursed because the music went static.

Gray noise. Falling rocks. *What fucking God?*

In the hotel bathroom my mother braids my wet hair, sits me on the toilet and explains how they drill into the mountains with big screws, drop sticks of dynamite into the holes they made.

In the next cut,
I imagine God
twisting a Phillips head to make the highway.

Sometimes he'd strip the screws, the metal shavings that sloughed off the silver that everybody's been mining for.

The radio is on its way out again,
Daddy grabs a novel from the dashboard
where he keeps them.
Black Hawk Down?
Or
Band of Brothers?
He snaps its spine.

At my great grandmother's funeral I practice her name in my head so that I don't forget when a grown up asks me how I'm doing. *Mémé, Mémé, Mémé, Janice.* In the hotel lobby the family gathers around. I focus on the snack machine and how my daddy has taught me to use size as advantage. My arm bends as a coat hanger might, I pluck PopTarts off the bottom row and hold them up proudly. My mother's family thinks I'm a delinquent and Daddy smiles big behind them.

We were on the way out of somewhere.
&

My mother bought me a coonskin cap on the Canadian border.
I let its tail stream down and lay alongside my braid.

I wore it when I stacked firewood for Daddy.

I wore it until I left it outside beside the fire pit. In the morning, the
chipmunks had torn it to pieces, ripped the coon's tail straight off its body.
Looking for protein, something to keep them warm.

&
My head felt the wind in throbs.

Nothing to keep my wet hair from icicling—
spears run down my back.
&
I imagined God had watched me
rub sticks together until I caught
a spark in my hand, then he laughed
so hard the fire ball got blown,

&
bounced down the road setting
fire to the neighbor's house.
They lost their dog and
it was God's fault.

Homeschooled, I watched the towers fall
on TV and couldn't understand
if the people air tumbling were falling or flying.

My mother let her tears water
the ficus trees in the sun-
room before shuffling Tori
and me into the Expedition.

We met my daddy at work and she let the radio
say it all: *fire; fire sky; smoke; smoking gun;*
collapse; America, keep your eyes on the sky.

When the towers fell my daddy was stripping
a house's siding clean off.
He was peeling it back bit by bit—scaly rubble
jewels sliding along the hill he worked on.

I heaved a piece of inch-thick
insulating foam over my head,
ran straight off that hill.

Flying until my parents weighed me down.

My family prepared for the apocalypse.
They anticipated rapture:

> Jim's Army Navy.   Gander
> Mountain.   Wal-Mart.   Sam's Club.
>   BUY IN BULK.
>   Water. Rice.

> Aluminum tape lining every door,
> every window. Pissing & shitting
> in the portable camping toilet upstairs.
>   Lessons on tightening canisters
>   of fresh air into our gas   masks.
> Cans of canned food   unzipped
>   quick with a Swiss Army knife.

Years later, imagine how we terrified the neighbors
when we finally emerged from the mountain. Imagine
how they must have taken our masks for monsters.

Imagine how fear can change a face forever.

When we got our first mountain
computer it was dial-up-ing forever
and all I wanted to do was sweet talk
dick pics, one from every state.
Wide dicks,

limp dicks, young and too-old dicks.
I collected.

I'd write things like:

fuck my O,

bite my breasts until
I bleed, come
save me,
take me
away from here.

And they'd always
respond in low resolution,
their dicks pixilated
but still
looking to me
like the last
branch to catch
before hitting
the ground.

My father's mother told me when I was 10 years old that she had an abortion
before my father took hold and I was lucky to be alive. My father and I were
both ungrateful. *Life isn't for everyone* is what she said.

This was after she fell
                 down
                        the elevator
                        shaft
                        and broke her back. Lumbar (concaved).
                                The lawsuit
                                cashed out millions.
                                            But I'm not supposed to write
                                          about all that.

This was after she taught
me how to roll a joint.
She said *No. That one's pregnant.*
They never smoke right.
Roll it out.

I have nothing
in my throat but death
and egg shells—
tonsil rock chitin.
When I cough,
I cough baby robins
that I drowned
in the womb of my mouth,
warm spit, red
wall, dark sea dive—
I don't know how to tell
lovers that my mouth,
my wet body with teeth,
is an empty nest.

//

my daddy, in the business of construction, ripped open / a million walls,
gutted them / pulled the pink insulation in strips, imagine some meaty /
intestines or baby back ribs / something that eats or can be eaten

//

fiber glass rock wool cellulose cancers / of lung meat blackening / this family
has a deep / history of emphysema & I've wrapped my lips / around so many
cigarettes my lungs are barrels of pressure / treated sawdust about to burst
red blackened blood / all over the new tongue & groove walls daddy built

//

& how my lover will squirm / when I cry out between the strikes / falling like
a house condemned might / *bend me over a sawhorse daddy*

//

In the beginning
I'd sniff poppers
and open up
for my lover.
We'd fuck each other
sopping and hum
into box fans to cool
the burn in the backs
of our throats.
We only knew
of inhalant orgasm.
We only knew
the way our bodies
would hot flash fast,
the way a deep breath
of dirty made it easy
to forget the details,
to approximate
absolutely everything
about each other,
until it felt just right.

At a museum that spiral staircases into the sky, my first lover's hand sweats inside of mine. This is where we belong, in the art. Christmas lights are wrapped around a woman who has been dead for years. Japanese men film themselves skating, harnessed and pulleyed, along canvases the size of sizable rooftops. Gutai, they call it.

Closer to the sky, there is a bathroom that's been turned into an electrical tape installation. I peel some from the walls and line her pockets. I slip into her and feel my fingers burn from the heat. Our hands sweat because they are all wrapped up.

We find a bed, in a backroom, and it's all chain-linked razor blades. My lover tugs my hand, like she does in Macy's or J. C. Penney's before we tumble onto a bed that's been made just for show, because we figure, why have a bed if it's not for lying.

The museum is dark, because in our minds, it is the middle of a new moon night. She leans me back toward the sharp bed, and the pain of being cut to pieces is lovely. I am nothing but myself sinking to the ground—still in love. She joins me beneath, makes a joke in what used to be my ear, whispers *we are the boogeywomen.*

When the blood of two women mixes it becomes deep
purple séance, maenad sacrifice, raw meat, abalone conch

shell you can hear the ocean in. It looks royal
from far away. When lovers have no bones,

                     things

                        grow complicated.

Velvet grows on antlers.
It grows there like moss, like ivy creeping up a wall.

When Daddy dropped deer out of season, he hit them
with spotlight spears and their eyes shone like sequins
sewn there—like the rhinestones Mom glued to Tori's dance costumes:
        Tap and jazz hands.
        Feet fast as hooves.
The stage lights would hit her hard and those sequins shone like eyes.

Mom taught me to costume myself,
taught me how to sew on my queen's skin when I wanted it:
Velvet, Lycra, sequins, leather. She called the stiches things like:
        Lazy daisy, fish bone, French, fly.
But she called me things like *Tom Boy* when I rolled in mud so thick the pill bugs
made maps of my skin—in the dirt caked there.
She called Tori things like:
        Performer, Princess, and *Off In La La Land.*

Antlers grow the finest velvet and my daddy
explained how, if you weren't careful,
they could *run you through,*
impale you, fuck you softly in the forest.

There are points to learning
and these are what I take:

Velvet grows on queen's skin. I shave it and sell it to black market queers because
I am a commodity:

        Buck out of season.

        Buck in rut.

        Cock in cunt.

Antlers are something sexed and I mount them

                          on my wall.

When my partner packs
their cock, the denim around them is a blue velvet
I take off in sheathes.

//

when i killed my first buck / daddy cut / its heart out & it was still /
pumping that black blood all over / it was gore sex /
the way it throbbed / hard in his hand

//

& i said *wow* / because i had never seen the inside / of something /
so clearly / i had never made something bleed / quite like that

//

not until i fucked / the first girl-woman / in the shower / & the first blood /
turned to peppermint / swirl in my palm / & the water ran / it away forever

//

& i said *wow* / because i had never made someone / bleed quite like that /
bleed just to bite / a *thank you* into my ear

the t-ball team blonde boy hits homeruns
and his aluminum baseball bat cracks my baby

      clitoris open
      splits seams
      and i throb out loud
      in my bed   facedown   for the first time
      my violin bow fingers slid and sliding

for the first time i dream bodies naked
six year old automaton dream bumble to spread my lips wide
find my cat-eye marble clit

and i look for blonde boy's too
search with mud pied fingers
through the layers of him

his clit is red white flame flare
dot of blood

in this dream our bodies are made of mirror
in this dream he becomes   something woman

Because my father's mother is a witch,
I have it in me too.

She listed ingredients.
Said: *this is how you kill a man:*

> *the baby you'll never have*
> *bone spur*
> *femur marrow*
> *a robin's blue shell crushed*
> *mange matted hair*
> *handful of wheat pennies*
> *dirt from the bed of a rat snake*
> *a lighter held under a teaspoon*
> *of your father's black blood*

She said *abra-come-dabra*
is how you make your lovers stay
longer, how you can make them
spill all over the floor.
They can't walk
away if they have no legs.

I only fall in love
with birds and Jersey
boys: Newark, Teaneck,
South, and Central, baby
robins fallen from a nest
of my hair, red-tailed hawk
on the mountain Mom
named Rusty, the couple
of bald eagles I learned
love from, holding hands
above the Susquehanna.

I want to be the witch of Endor
and necromance the doe's jaw
bone I keep necklaced at my throat.

I want to have a long conversation
in which this dead, omnivorous,

girl admits how badly she wants to clamp
down and taste the way my jugular blood

pumps like the best sex she's ever had.

I want to speak exclusively with women

who do not begin the day wanting me.

I want to show them

what it feels like

to taste blood

and like it.

Back Mountain Dance Studio

My mother waits for Tori to be done tapping and chats with the other mothers. My mother is by far the prettiest but only really knows it on Wednesdays, because on Wednesdays she sneaks a belly dancing class from my father. She jangles, thin coins chandeliering up her hips. My mother is everything if you're looking close enough. The mothers in the waiting room compare the messes that mount in their purses. They complain about husbands who limp, husbands who are gay, they complain about the roses they tattooed on their tits at 17 looking like melted lipstick at the bottom of their purses. My mother chooses to only see the bright side and opens the waiting room blinds, lets the streetlights spark up the snow and slip in. The other mothers hate how good she looks in cold light and don't think at all about what that might mean. Her eyes crystal— beneath them blue.

Tunkhannock Softball Bleachers

My mother waits for the last inning of every game, drums her fingers with anxiety because my mother is the mother of a dyke that wants to fuck the other mother's daughters. To them this makes my mother the devil, and these good Christian women are hostile when facing a devil. Sometimes I imagine my mother pronged and dangerous, and she looks good. The mothers imagine my mother requested a pitchfork as her IV when she labored me out. The mothers smartly deduce that it is mostly my mother's fault that I exist. The mothers hate that I am the best on the diamond, that I am studded with diamonds and spin circles around their daughters like a saw blade. They hate that I fuck every daughter, that I make each one come to the dark side. And every mother blames my mother and not the way it's really my arms that pitchfork at each end, the way I burn, right out in the open.

At night I ride
my mouth
down the road
to her nipple.
I let it in
and keep it
there. I know
how this seems.
To suckle this late
in life is oedipal.
I know that
the way I love
women has always
been wrong.
My dreams are all
milk and come
and my teeth
falling out.

the 911 operator asks me the riddle of the sphinx / i recite my address and imagine lights strobing across mist-blue pyramids / appalachia in twilight / how many ways can you slice history / watch its arteries spill reds in the bathtub / my father dies this way / his urned ashes already tickle my nose / i have no imagination but foresight

the sphinx visits my bathroom / stretches her stiff / stony legs / and looks upon my father / she spits yellow bile into the wastebasket filled with strawberry caps / cherry pits / razor blades / she vomits the oedipal answer

|| man || man || man ||

When my daddy caught his cold, it lasted forever. He never left his bed—back flat, eyes all white and up on the ceiling. He'd take Imodium to stop up and he'd piss in Gatorade bottles. Often, the caps would slip into the tangles of sweat-in sheets.

The smell of urine kicked the back of my throat until I coughed up childhood. My mother would say of her bedroom:

it's just so hard to breathe in there.

Sometimes, when he did move, he'd kick the red-brown jugs over, watch as it rivered out. He'd watch and let the sourness seep into the plywood floors for later.

Mountains form below the surface.

&

make hills to camp in.

We drive a rented trailer into a camp of trailers. I run off with a boy about my age and he falls and skins his knees. He says it will make him feel better and he will give me Legos if I hold his penis in my hand for a whole minute counting *Mississippi* and I can't believe that they use *Mississippi* even this far north. So I do and he gave me the Legos in a Ziploc bag but when I try to build with them, I realize he's melted each piece with the lighter he stole from his mother who smokes too many cigarettes. Nothing fits together, they're all too warped. Some are stretched to sharpness, spears, plastic ice in primary colors.

In the next town, we want eggs for breakfast.
The waitress tells us there was a murder down the road.
They found the body this morning. My daddy scoffs as she says:

Our little town. Startin' to be Godless.

And as we leave the town we drive past a house
all roped off.
Victorian thing. Paint chipped.

A monarch butterfly
hits the windshield.
Wipers take its wings

&

spread them like pollen.
We were on our way out.

From the back seat, it's as if the semis
drive themselves.

Truckers are ghosts after the sun starts setting.
I tell my mother.
&
my mother says

I know. That's why I can see them.
My daddy sleeps, head back, throat like mountain
ridges. Falling rock. Gray noise.

Ectoplasm.
She tunes to the trucker's station.
Channel 19. East coast. Soft static.

Do ghosts sleep?
I ask my mother.
&
she mumbles things in CB code:

back row,
commercial company,
lot lizard,
sleeper creeper,

male buffalo,

        having shutter trouble,

&

she pats my daddy unconcious on his thigh
said: *They sleep.*

They sleep all the time.

I imagine my daddy's mind
looks most like broken

dryer machines
scattered in a forest,

field mice living
in the leftover lint.

I imagine it looks
like stepped-on

syringes, too,
flies stooping

down to sop up
all the sweet.

She says,   *I am tired of this*
                   mountain. My hands
                   are so cold I'm afraid
                   they'll icicle-break
                   at the wrist. I'm afraid
                   I'll be left with no
                   way to hold.

She says,   *I need rock salt to melt*
                   this ice. I need to chain-
                   wrap these tires. Kayla,
                   we need to drive away.

She says,   *But I still love him*

                              and cries into her
                              frostbitten hands.
                              And her sea salt tears
                              warm them, thaw them
                              back to life, thaw them

                                     enough for a short drive

                                     and then straight back

                                     up the mountain.

my mother was good at cooking birds / chicken &
cornish hens & grouse & wild turkey / at 11 i'd 22
caliber turkeys / i'd pluck them until i poke prodded
myself to bleed / bled until i blowtorched the
smooth downy feathers right off /

mom learned to cook at the same pace i learned to
kill / & she learned to flavor the tasteless / tenderize
the tough / she'd shoot the bird up / inject it with
fire taste / she could always make more of less /

my mother shot fire drugs into daddy too / when
he asked for it / & as his eyes rolled to white cloud
/ my mother saw the bright side / said *you carve it
this time* / & as she passed me the sharpest knife /
she'd say:

|| serrate || serrate || serrate ||

//

In the 50s my mother's mother balanced jugs of water on her head in Algiers and her father preached. He was kidnapped by Algerian soldiers, gone for 40 days and 40 nights.

//

Biblically speaking, daughters are often silently upset with their fathers.

//

My mother's mother talks about climbing trees with her brother. They would split hard-boiled eggs up there, she the white and he the yolk.

//

The neighbor boy and I hunted dragons, newts, toads, frogs. We waded out knee high, black silt between our toes. We used sand buckets and gold miners' sieves to haul in a harvest of frog eggs— bundles of slippery eyes. We stole from every amphibious mother.

We did not think of how our mothers would have felt if we had been abducted at that Memorial Day baseball game, like we almost had. We did not think it cruel to squeeze the eggs between our fingers until they popped, like concord grapes.

Potential energy means nothing to children.

As I wiped a hundred could have been tadpoles on my ripped tye-dye shirt, the neighbor boy laughed at the mess, pointed to the wet smudges. He announced my ovaries and told me I would make a terrible mother, announced both fertility and maternal ineptitude—an equation that cancels itself out.

There is nothing political in thinking of what could have been. Abort everything you must.

But still, if I cut my breasts off with a scalpel, as I do in nearly every dream, will milk pour out? Will the ghosts of a hundred frogs open their mouths and coil their tongues around a steady stream? Will the children I'll never have demand their *could have been* mother's body back?

Things try to crawl out
of me and I let them ooze
dance down my leg, hold
their hands as they drip.
I collect cysts and lance
them with needles from gas
stations, burn the tip to sterility.
I know every needle's purpose.
I tell the needle right to its face
that it will never be clean
after being inside me.
When the surgeon ripped me
open, she said she'd cut
the hate out. She said it ran
like a rope along my groin.
She said it was coming
for my cunt.

me and tori licked food stamps when we were young because we liked the way poverty tasted and we were hungry. we always wore the same outfits to the dhr office: me a black tattered goodwill sweater, the zodiac signs spinning in teal like a twister board. tori wore ███████████
████████████████. we stuck our lower lips out like beggars' cups and the women who worked for the state tucked cans of canned peached and jars of pickles into our inner lips like snuff. we kept them there for the harder winter months, and then we ate them all at once and burned ourselves to acid reflux. on fire, we imagined how good it would feel

     if the fire station shoved
     hoses down our throats.

        daddy had pride in his blood so he tried to stoke ours and
        make up for all the canned peaches. he pointed to the rings
        moon-cratering our tongues. he named them what they
        were: *mediterranean.* he told us it was in our blood

          to be malnourished.

In early Autumn I'd fire up the woodstove and feed it
infestations of everything. I'd exterminate the house,

rip the silverware drawer from its track and choke
the stove with the carpenter ants that crawled there.

I'd toss in sprung rat traps and shovel in the still wet
wood I had hauled, ripe with termites and wood worms.

By Halloween all we smelled was apple cider
and burning bark. The vat of cider boiled

from October on and my mother would toss
in citruses, cranberries, cinnamon sticks. I'd contribute

ears: deer, fox, coyote. Sometimes their whole faces, ripped
into masks. Sometimes my own. Red-blooded, it burned

hard on the way down.

i spent years sticking my tongue
into the heads of venus

fly traps just to feel
the bite of someone else

because i knew that was the only
way to really grow up

my first lover bit my neck
until it bruised because i had put myself

in her mouth and explained
why carnivorous plants are the most beautiful

i said *i want to make you*
the top of the food chain

i want you to teeth
flex into me

molar vice me down
don't let me

move and that was the year i learned
that some plants in south

america could swallow animals whole
::rat::bird::housecat::pussy::

so i put mine on a platter
offered it up

said *chew your food*

daddy played chicken with the neighbor's dog
because he didn't like the way it barked.

when we drove by daddy'd
swerve chase it into the ground

                                'till it pulped.

he'd laugh as the dust kicked up behind us.
he'd say *he's gonna be out for awhile.*

daddy ran that dog down three times
with me in the passenger seat
he crush-maimed it
he crush-maimed it
he crush-maimed it

and then daddy'd get mad when the dog
got better, get mad when the dog
barked the same as it had before.

that neighbor's house burnt down
eventually, all the way to cinder block
foundation and that fire took the dog down
with it. daddy laughed from the driver's seat
and the back of his throat smelled
of dirt roads and spent matches.

let's imagine that as an
adult
my spine is a road

broken
line
passing
lane
vertebrae

& i beg to be run over

& the one who drives
drives me with a flogger—
their hot new whip

& let's imagine the
holes I let them bore,
deep, dark puddles
of blue bruise.
& let's count
how many
black
holes
a body
can hold

before it hyper
novas to blue brightness
& let's just call me what I
am:

degenerative star

put a collar on me
and I'll bark
or hang myself
from your belt loop
to become
your animal
is to become
less and at the same time
more

in the house on the hill
we hung coyotes on the wall
and our lab bark-whimpered,
confusing them for mirrors,
or oracles, maybe even, a premonition
of a strung up future.

they hung there and i pet them, combed
them for summer shed that wouldn't come.

i've never seen a wolf
in the wild. elusive dog.

but i've seen bears, bobcats, & lions
built exclusively for the mountain,
appalachian cats—
sphinxes riddling away at me,
boring holes.
& daddy was always taking shots
out the window
exploding them
to rorschach.

planetary the way my partner moves
around me—skirt—elliptical—
they name me *mountain*
from a distance, drop
dynamite into the cliff hangs
of my shoulder blades, lumbar
fractured out—vertebrae, bone slide.
if we ever align, they sieve. pluck
from the rubble glue
covered rhinestones,
pyrite foolishly golden, ruby
flecks from where my body
caves—rock // cut—
my partner's rough mining hands
the highway trucking through.

When me and the one
     who whips me

         talk about sex

   we speak in switch,
     say things like:

   Skies flare   like match   tips
        when I strangle   swans.

   Beneath wringing fingers,
     they death-squawk

        into oranging horizon.

   & I recall
   the cocks   I wrapped

   my lips around,   stiff as swan
       spines   rubbed

   on my tongue. Squeezed,
   they limp   in my mouth,

      their necks' white
      feathers smoothed   down.

When they die,
they die exhausted.

       I string them   up in braided
            cords,   shibari rope   them

            to splintery   beams—
            chandeliers   that spin light

       to the walls   like the fast
            flung webs   of black   spiders.

       I hunt them,
       the swans,
       stalk-straddle   them

       into submission.   They thrash
       and gasp   for my throat—

       my esophageal   kiss-grip.
       I swallow   their   last breaths.

When we die, babe,
we die exhausted.

The fact that my father beat me has nothing to do with the fact that my ex-lover did, that my lover does.

The fact that my father beat me has nothing to do with the fact that my ex-lover did, that my lover does.

The fact that my father beat me has nothing to do with the fact that my ex-lover did, that my lover does.

Each smack is singular.
Each fist is something new.

If I count the reasons in order:

                             Zero.

                             Infidelity.

                             Begging for it.
                             On my knees for it.

I want to write
about a color.
Let me say:
my violet body
is violet because
you made it
so. But violet is just
purple. Instead,
let me say:
my violent body
is just a purple
reaction. If you get out
what you put in,
is my body phallic
now? Violet cock.
It's spring again.
Always is. Fists
watering flowers
built to spit back.

i say crucify me
to the white birch
out back, babe.

the way its bark peels
is how i want to be peeled.
flay the fuck outta me

& babe, don't mistake my sex
for sacrilege. this is my religion
spilling, this is my religious coming.

I've got god between my legs.

kneel, babe.

reach in and pray with me.
reach in and touch the red
smooth cloud where I keep my god.

this faith is deep
and I want you
to have some.

don't ever wash
your hands of it

If I am too vainglorious during sex call me Cassiopeia and punish me in rope work.

String me to the ceiling and let me hang upside down for half the year. Watch me carefully.

The blood will rush to my face like a falling theater curtain. But know that the show's not over.

Our scenes are give and take. My blood runs back and forth and sounds most like a rain stick.

You always understand this. And you understand that I will ask you to do unspeakable things.

I will look at your crude knots tethering me to the sky and I will demand you to do better

because I am the most beautiful woman in the world. I will say, *If you want to punish me*

right, kill my father's mother. Rip out her varicose veins. Start Achilles and work

your way up from there. She won't be my blood anymore if you empty her. Whisper

in my ear that her blood flowed backward until she begged for mercy. Tell me how

you did not give her any mercy. Tell me again that I am the most beautiful woman.

I'll come hard and constellate all over myself.

what if, somewhere in the course
of this story, i rename myself?
what if i say, *now call me kayleb?*

what if i said that god told me
to look for the promised land
& i fingered myself

until deciding
that my clitoris is penal
in its confidence.

my story is nothing if not
in search of something
& it can't be sacrilege

if i get off, if i prayer chant
each pleasure. it can't be sacrilege
if i'm devout, at least to myself.

I collect holy books
and burn them

        in the backyard,

                roll in what's left
                until I am a painted god.

    This is not my normal
narcissism. This is what I look like
when I'm trying to save myself.

my boy tits
slam against the pulpit and slip off

      to become

            the body of Christ
            my body of Christ
            my body of Christ

              wafting
             down

            I'm lighter now

&

i've decided
my body is evil,

and evilly religious—
it climaxes in tongues

when my lip   stick   is blue

                                i look

in the mirror   &   pronounce myself

            deadboy::ashgray::sleepingbeauty::coldasice

        i necromance myself

    just to say   *necrophilia*
                                       has never seemed
                                       so hot

                dead name me

                            baby   i want

            to rip you
            limb from limb

the hair mounding between my legs
makes me dwell on my lycanthropy

i black out and remember nothing
of what the neighbor boys leave

tangled there // candy wrappers fool's
gold the silver head of a cotton mouth

their blood and mine // sperm that isn't
yet sperm and so it's un-listable

i imagine myself in this black lapse
(all wolf) falsely lustful and gnashing

i want to eat them wholly
and wake up as what I eat

I catch lymphomania and roll
my fingers along my partner,
        beneath their breasts,
        over them, above them

until I trace gold leaf clavicle
until I'm lost in the valleys of under arm.

I'm looking for frozen peas, marbles, *something irregular*
on a body not made of regular. I'm looking for heredity,
faulty inheritance. I'm looking for family.

        My partner checks my breasts
        and finds addiction,
        cuts it out careful with their tongue.

They spit and run it down the sink.

I collect antique photographs: tin type, sepia, glass slides. I hang them everywhere I go because I want to rebuild my family tree from the top down, and I take comfort in the way they poltergeist-rattle on the walls, sounding like my parents used to—pacing above me, sexing above me— their feet and genitals thud-splintering on our unfinished plywood floors.

I only find my family in what's not mine: estate sale, stranger's home under dust, a Ouija board for sale and spinning like a compass   until

it stops and points me toward an 1800s cash drawer.

The Ouija whispers:
ashes to ashes, dust to dust.

And inside, no money
but my ancestor's
cremated remains.

Each suicide its own coin pocket.
Each addict flame dried
into their own shallow grave.

I do what anyone would do.
I roll a twenty into my nose

and blow.

When my mother chewed off
her own hands it was because
she convinced herself each finger
was the penis of a man
who would have treated her
better. She would tick
them off as she sucked
and chewed:

> *X, and X, and X,*
> *and he's a lawyer now,*
> *and he's a business owner,*
> *and the other's just plain kind.*

She would hum while she fellated
each little bit of herself. And every
mistake she'd ever made would swell
in her mouth before its castration.

When my daddy ripped the wedding ring
off my mother's last remaining finger
he threw it into the forest.

For years, I thought I saw it glinting there,
until my mother opened her mouth to cry

out for help, until I saw that that ring
had landed inside her, until I saw it

   vice-clamp-cock-ringed
   around her esophagus.

Until I heard nothing at all from her,
because it's hard to talk without your hands.

as a child i made lists / i made lists of meat and meaty parts / my mother would caldron catch me stirring rabbit's feet, my dog's clipped toenails, beaks of turkey and grouse, the liver of a fawn daddy killed out of season / daddy'd say, *the young ones are so tender* / and i'd keep stirring and my mother started to worry that i wasn't getting enough sun, that all the meat i ate was just a little too green to be good / she said *what's wrong with you* and i poured her an elixir / i said *here mommy, this is for you and me, it will invisible us, it will make daddy wonder where we've gone to / mommy, this is the good drink* / she humored me, took the glass-vialed potion and put it on a shelf of birthday party sand arts / and it sat there and it sat there and it rotted through the glass and it acid tore through each floor and me and mommy lava jumped through the living room right before the whole damn house burnt down with daddy still in it / and after i took mommy's hand, said, pointing to only ash, *see? invisible.*

At the base of the mountain there was water, a cavern-lake stocked
with palm-sized rainbow fish, empty beer cans, bullet casings. It caught
all the family's runoff; it was a pool of our dirty groundswell.

Along the water's edge, Daddy taught me to hook worms, run them through
lengthwise so they had no hope. He called it a *butt fuck*, and licked
the worm dirt off his fingers after. He said it tasted *like faggots*
and I felt my body tighten, contract around something unnamable.

The fish we caught were doomed cause Daddy didn't believe in catch
and release so he cut their heads off with the cleaver he carried. Butcher-Daddy
topped the food chain. He juggled those fish heads and when his hands were red-
painted he left their fleshy skulls piled on the mountain as a pyramid. Daddy
said the little mound of death was just what the doctor ordered.

Daddy couldn't stop himself, so he shot the turkey vultures that came
for those kaleidoscoping fish heads. Daddy never wanted to stop
so he noosed those birds by their long necks and cut the throats
of the bears that pawed their tar-feather corpses.

Daddy was on top of the mountain. Daddy coughed out commandments
and kept the ecosystem in his mouth for safekeeping. Daddy was genesis
and judgment day. Daddy was surprised when our whole world went extinct.

Now, in AA meetings, I call myself *Kayleb* and talk about the true order of things.
I say, *This is who eats what.* I say, *Look who's on top. It never fucking changes.*
I say, *I've never drunk all of the promised land at once like Daddy-God asked*
because I always black out or vomit first. I say, *My vomit is a pile of fish heads*
and never rainbows or refracts a damn thing.

I drink when I want to be fucked in the ass like a real man,
when I want forget everything about who's on top, chain-binding me down.

to understand the scope
of my father's heart
imagine it

easily wrapped in the legs
of a daddy long leg
spider imagine

that there is a whole
lot of daddy
leg to spare

imagine killing that spider
with the sword-
head of a pin

envision it
post-post mortem
rigor mortis-curled

around its own corpse
—a lonesome
embrace

imagine that in this instance
of formaldehyde
my father is at his most alive

and to understand the strength
of my father's heart
compare it

to a restaurant lobby
claw-machine tendriling
for attention

compare being a part
of my father's heart

to being dropped again
and again by that claw

I went back to the mountain for my sister
but she wanted to stay

delirious in our bedroom
petting the shed rat snake skin
the house falling down
around her and her laughing
and her laughing
and her pointing to my bedside,

where I'd left a glass half empty.

A mouse drowned facedown, its front
bloated and flaking green flesh,
it's two back feet skeletal.

I left her there.

Now, in late summers, animals die
under piles of the first fallen leaves
and I can name them by nose:

Mus musculus
Rattus
Sciuridae
Sister.

my daddy who art
in the hawaiian
islands and neck
deep in his own
neurosis stole my sister
flew   under the cover
of fatherhood
until no one knew
where to look
until the shock
of a missing child
ebbed to dull
thuds in the backs
of our throats
lost and
lozenge
lozenge

On the mountain
        we used to feed each other
                bullets to say I love you.

We used to walk around with
        mouthfuls of slugs and feel weighed
                deep down into the dirt.

My family is so far
        apart now I can only
                reach them by bullet.

I check my wristwatch and take
        the curvature of the earth
                into consideration.

I feed lead into my rifle's
        chamber and each round
                has a name I chant.

                      :: Victoria :: Tori ::
                      :: Peter :: Jerome ::
                      :: Neives :: Your Lady of the Snows ::
                      :: Our Lady of Sorrows ::

I shoot over a continent.
I sniper find them.

I walk to the gulf
to taste their blood in the water.

I know they're thinking of me,
lighting all my names on fire, too.

The last deer I reach for meets
the front of a metro north. She decorates
its grill in red tendon sinew
and my mouth waters for venison again.
Hunger is all the woods left in me.

I want to eat everything that's ever happened to me.

I'll fire it up on the grill.
I'll serve it up still bloody.

ACKNOWLEDGMENTS

A special thanks to the publications that gave some of these pages their first homes, in various forms, and under different names: *Booth, Connotation Press, Cutbank, theEEEL, Fourteen Hills, The Grief Diaries, Muzzle, No Tokens, Puerto del Sol, Smoking Glue Gun, Vinyl Poetry, The Wanderer,* and *Zymbol.*

Thank you to KMA Sullivan and the whole YesYes team for making this dream come true. And a special thanks to Phillip B. Williams for introducing me to YesYes Books in Minneapolis back in 2014. That meeting changed the course of my life in the best way. Thank you Stevie Edwards, for believing in my work on so many different occasions, and always advocating for me. Thank you Jill Kolongowski for being understanding, organized, and as inspired by magic as I am.

A special thanks to all the writers whose work I so admire and look to for inspiration: sam sax, Kaveh Akbar, T Clutch Fleischmann, Aziza Barnes, TC Tolbert, Jayson Smith, Cortney Lamar Charleston, Justin Phillip Reed, Safia Elhillo, Danez Smith, jayy dodd, Paul Tran, C. Russell Price, Tiana Clark, Thiahera Nurse, and so, so many others. I read y'all when I've forgotten myself and need reminding.

Thank you to the 2015 Lambda Literary Emerging Nonfiction fellows for looking at thirteen pages of this manuscript and telling me to write sixty more. Your confidence in this project allowed it to truly be born.

Thank you to Yutha Adiputra Yamanaka for this beautiful cover art. As soon as I saw this work, I felt such a deep harmony.

A mountain of gratitude and love to my friends and support system: Kit Emslie, Shaelyn Smith, Rachel Dispenza, Diamond Forde, Rebecca Brown, Nabila Lovelace, Erik Kline, Rachel Brown, shelley feller, Reem Abu-Baker, Aqua Dublavee, Grant TerBush, Geoffrey Emerson, Lizzie Smith Emerson, and so many others. You all breathe such bright light into my life.

Thank you to Bob, Billa, Sides, Skinner, Austin, and Egans Bar for giving me a home away from home and making it a safe and welcoming space to write, play, and just exist.

Thank you to my teachers: Camille-Yvette Welsch, Julia Kasdorf, Robin Becker, Charlotte Holmes, Toni Jensen, Christopher Reed, Michael Martone, L. Lamar Wilson, Hali Felt, Wendy Rawlings, and many others. Your faith in me started long before I had begun to earn it.

Thank you to every student I've ever had the privilege of instructing. You taught me so much about writing and about kindness—even how to marry the two. Spending time learning with all of you has been such a blessing.

All my love and thanks to Joshua Sanders, Amy Horrigan, and Lauren Auriemma. Your love has made my life so damn fun, and though distance and circumstance might interrupt our friendships, it's so strengthening to know you are, and will continue to be, bright and beautiful constants in my life.

Thank you, Nana, for continuing to teach me about forgiveness, and forgiving me again and again as I am slow to learn. I am happy to have you in my life.

Thank you, Grandmommy, for supporting my art and my education at every turn. I wouldn't have half of what I have without you. Thank you for seeing me, and seeing me through.

Thank you, Momma Bear, for keeping us alive on that mountain, and keeping us alive long enough to get off that mountain. Without you I wouldn't be around to write anything at all and now, finally, I am so incredibly happy to be alive. There is really no way to express the love and appreciation I feel for you, but hopefully this book got close.

And finally, a whole heart of thank yous to Jack Papanier, my person in this world. You opened my eyes to all the beauty I was missing. You whispered opal. You called me by my true name. You became my first and only real home.

You told me I never belonged to that mountain, and I feel so much better now.

All light floats.
All light is always floating.

FULL-LENGTH COLLECTIONS

i be, but i ain't by Aziza Barnes

The Feeder by Jennifer Jackson Berry

Love the Stranger by Jay Deshpande

Blues Triumphant by Jonterri Gadson

North of Order by Nicholas Gulig

Meet Me Here at Dawn by Sophie Klahr

I Don't Mind If You're Feeling Alone by Thomas Patrick Levy

If I Should Say I Have Hope by Lynn Melnick

Landscape with Sex and Violence by Lynn Melnick

some planet by jamie mortara

Boyishly by Tanya Olson

Pelican by Emily O'Neill

The Youngest Butcher in Illinois by Robert Ostrom

A New Language for Falling Out of Love by Meghan Privitello

I'm So Fine: A List of Famous Men & What I Had On by Khadijah Queen

American Barricade by Danniel Schoonebeek

The Anatomist by Taryn Schwilling

Gilt by Raena Shirali

Panic Attack, USA by Nate Slawson

[insert] boy by Danez Smith

Man vs Sky by Corey Zeller

The Bones of Us by J. Bradley
   [Art by Adam Scott Mazer]

CHAPBOOK COLLECTIONS

VINYL 45S
After by Fatimah Asghar
Inside My Electric City by Caylin Capra-Thomas
Dream with a Glass Chamber by Aricka Foreman
Pepper Girl by Jonterri Gadson
Of Darkness and Tumbling by Mónica Gomery
Bad Star by Rebecca Hazelton
Makeshift Cathedral by Peter LaBerge
Still, the Shore by Keith Leonard
Please Don't Leave Me Scarlett Johansson by Thomas Patrick Levy
Juned by Jenn Marie Nunes
A History of Flamboyance by Justin Phillip Reed
No by Ocean Vuong
This American Ghost by Michael Wasson

BLUE NOTE EDITIONS
Beastgirl & Other Origin Myths by Elizabeth Acevedo
Kissing Caskets by Mahogany L. Browne

COMPANION SERIES
Inadequate Grave by Brandon Courtney
The Rest of the Body by Jay Deshpande